Charli and the Christmas Bush

Leanne Murner

Illustrated by Kat Fox

Serenity Press Pty Ltd
Waikiki, WA 6169

First published by Serenity Press (Serenity Press Kids) in 2021
www.serenitypress.org

Copyright © Leanne Murner 2021

All rights reserved. No part of this publication may be reproduced, stored in a retrieval system, or transmitted in any form or by any means, electronic, mechanical, photocopying, recording or otherwise, without the prior written permission of the publisher.

National Library of Australia
Cataloguing in-Publication entry

Murner, Leanne (Leanne, Murner), Charli and the Christmas Bush

ISBN: 978-0-6451762-3-0 (sc)
ISBN: 978-0-6451762-2-3 (hc)
ISBN: 978-0-6451762-4-7 (e)

Copyright © Cover and illustrations by Kat Fox

Charli and the Christmas Bush

Leanne Murner

Illustrated by Kat Fox

"Hey, Poppy John, what are you doing?" asked Charli.

"I am cutting some Christmas Bush to make a table decoration for Christmas Day," said Poppy John.

"Why is it called a Christmas Bush?"

"Because they flower just before Christmas," he said.

"Did you want to help me?"

"Oh yes please," said Charli.

"Oh Poppy, what are all those butterflies doing up there?" Charli asked.

"Butterflies drink the nectar from the flowers and they also lay their eggs on the leaves that will then hatch into caterpillars," said Poppy John.

"See here, Charli, these leaves have some eggs on them. We will make sure we leave them so the eggs can hatch," said Poppy John.

"There are lots of birds that like the Christmas Bush too, because of the dense bush-like branches. Birds can hide in there and make their nests and feed on all the insects that the bush attracts," said Poppy John.

"Oh look, Poppy, is that a bird nest there? What sort of bird is that?" said Charli.

"That bird is the Fairy Wren, its nest is a dome with two holes to go in and out. Can you see that little head poking out? If you look up there, there is also a Tawny Frogmouth."

"Oh yeah, Poppy, I can see it!" said Charli.

"Let's go and make these decorations," said Poppy.

"Oh Poppy, I would love to have one of those Christmas Bushes at my place," Charli said.

"Oh, wouldn't that be great, then you can make Christmas decorations with the flowers every year," said Poppy John.

"And I can have the butterflies laying their eggs and the birds nesting too."

"Okay, Charli, it's bedtime, let's put out some cookies and milk for Santa and some gum leaves for the reindeer, said Poppy John.

"I hope Santa brings me a Christmas Bush just like yours, Poppy!" said Charli.

Poppy John smiled. "You will just need to wait and see in the morning."

"Goodnight Poppy."

"Goodnight Charli."

"Poppy! Poppy! Look! My very own Christmas Bush!" said Charli on Christmas Day. "Mum, look what I got!"

"Oh, wow Charli, that will look great in our garden," said Mum.

"Merry Christmas, Charli," said Poppy.

"Can you help me get the decorations for the table?" he asked.

"I will get them, Poppy!"

"Oh Charli, these look great," said Poppy. "I could not have done them without your help!"

"Oh Charli, you are very lucky to now have your own Christmas Bush," said Mum.

"I am going to look after it so all the insects and birds can have their home at our place," said Charli.

Christmas Bush

The NSW Christmas bush is a tree as well as a small shrub. It is unique in that its petals are not the brightest and most beautiful part of the plant. That feat instead goes to the vibrantly coloured sepals that emerge after flowering and become bold and bright in colour. After flowering in spring, the tree will begin to gradually decorate itself by turning a bright scarlet red just before Christmas.

To achieve the brightest red coloured sepals, plant your Christmas bush in a sun-drenched spot. They work best in a bush garden setting, or as a screening plant, and their creamy white flowers attract native butterflies, moths and bees.

Butterfly (Purple Copper)

The purple copper butterfly is only found in the Central Tablelands of NSW. Its habitat is restricted to elevations above 900 metres. The purple copper butterfly is a small butterfly with a thick body, and a wingspan of only 20-30 millimetres. The upper sides of its wings are black or deep brown, with a bronze or green iridescence when they are sunning. Its black antennae are dotted with white spots and terminate with a black tip.

Adult males fly rapidly at about 1 metre from the ground and rest in the sun with their wings parted. Females fly less rapidly and tend to stay closer to the host plant. Adults usually fly on warm cloudless days in September, around the middle of the day.

Fairy Wren

Adult male Superb Fairy-wrens are among the most brightly coloured of the species, especially during the breeding season. They have rich blue and black plumage above and on the throat. The belly is grey-white, and the bill is black. Females and young birds are mostly brown above with a dull red-orange area around the eye and a brown bill. Females have a pale greenish gloss, absent in young birds, on the otherwise brown tail. Several other species of fairy-wren are found in Australia. The males of each species are quite distinct, but the females and young birds are often difficult to separate.

Superb Fairy-wrens feed on insects and other small arthropods. These are caught mostly on the ground but may also be taken from low bushes. Feeding takes place in small social groups.

The nest is a dome-shaped structure of grasses and other fine material. It is usually placed in a low bush and is constructed by the female. The female incubates the eggs alone, but both sexes feed the young. Other members of the group will also help with the feeding of the young.

Tawny Frogmouth

The tawny frogmouth is a species of frogmouth native to the Australian mainland and Tasmania and found throughout. It is a big-headed, stocky bird, often mistaken for an owl, due to its nocturnal habits and similar colouring.

They can be found in almost any habitat type, including forests and woodlands, scrub and heathland vegetation, and savannahs. They are seen in large numbers in areas populated with many river gums and casuarinas, and can be found along river courses if these areas are timbered. Tawny frogmouths are common in suburbs, having adapted to human presence. They have been reported nesting in parks and gardens with trees.

Tawny frogmouths are carnivorous and are considered to be among Australia's most effective pest-control birds, as their diet consists largely of species regarded as vermin or pests in houses, farms, and gardens. The bulk of their diet is composed of large nocturnal insects, such as moths, as well as spiders, worms, slugs, and snails.

The clutch size of the tawny frogmouth is one to three eggs. Both sexes share incubation of the eggs during the night, whilst during the day, males incubate the eggs.

Dedication

I would like to dedicate this book to my best friend and husband. Thank you for supporting me through this amazing journey.

My niece Charli for being my inspiration, Poppy John for his wealth of knowledge and support.

And to my amazing friend Amy for pushing me out of my comfort zone two years ago, starting my new life purpose.

I would not be here today without you believing in me.

About the Author

Leanne Murner is an author, business owner/designer at 5 Little Bears Pty Ltd and a proud mum of five boys. Leanne saw a gap in the market for Australian themed wooden toys and began creating products for children with an educational and Australian twist. Being a creative soul Leanne grew the business fast and as time went by her product portfolio increased. In addition she has also published the first two of a series of six children's books, Franki and the Banskia, and Loui and the Grass Tree, with the remaining being published this year. Leanne wanted to teach kids about Australian native flora and fauna, what they are and who needs them to survive. Leanne is busy working on another series of books teaching kids about Australian animals and their habitat, threats and how we can help. Leanne is passionate that our children need to be better educated on Australian wildlife to help keep it from extinction.

www.ingramcontent.com/pod-product-compliance
Lightning Source LLC
Chambersburg PA
CBHW041412160426
42811CB00107B/1767